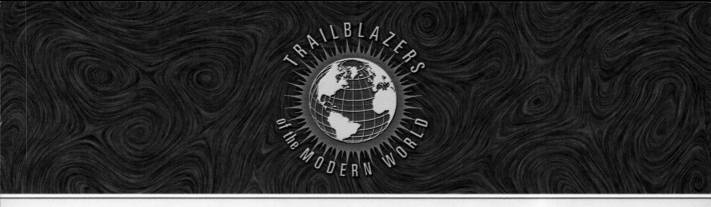

MUHAMMAD ALI

By James Buckley Jr.

WORLD ALMANAC® LIBRARY

Please visit our web site at: www.worldalmanaclibrary.com
For a free color catalog describing World Almanac® Library's list
of high-quality books and multimedia programs, call 1-800-848-2928 (USA)
or 1-800-387-3178 (Canada). World Almanac® Library's fax: (414) 332-3567.

Library of Congress Cataloging-in-Publication Data

Buckley, James, 1963-
    Muhammad Ali / by James Buckley, Jr.
        p. cm. — (Trailblazers of the modern world)
    Includes bibliographical references and index.
    Summary: A biography of the legendary boxer, who began his career as Cassius Clay, discussing his prowess
in the ring, his conversion to Islam and opposition to the Vietnam War, and his life after boxing.
    ISBN 0-8368-5096-3 (lib. bdg.)
    ISBN 0-8368-5256-7 (softcover)
    1. Ali, Muhammad, 1942—Juvenile literature. 2. Boxers (Sports)—United States—Biography—Juvenile
literature. [1. Ali, Muhammad, 1942- . 2. Boxers (Sports). 3. African Americans—Biography.] I. Title.
II. Series.
GV1132.A44B83   2004
796.83'092—dc22
[B]   2003061790

First published in 2004 by
World Almanac® Library
330 West Olive Street, Suite 100
Milwaukee, WI 53212 USA

Project manager: Jonny Brown
Editor: Jim Mezzanotte
Design and page production: Scott M. Krall
Photo research: Diane Laska-Swanke
Indexer: Walter Kronenberg

Photo credits: © AP/Wide World Photos: cover, 6, 12, 15, 20, 21 bottom, 24, 29, 30 top, 40, 41 both, 43;
© Bettmann/CORBIS: 7, 8, 10, 17, 26, 33 bottom, 34, 37; © Michael Brennan/CORBIS: 38; © Jerry
Cooke/CORBIS: 4; © Michael Cooper/Getty Images: 42; © The Courier-Journal: 9; © David J. &
Janice L. Frent Collection/CORBIS: 22; © Dirck Halstead/Getty Images: 39; © Hulton Archive: 13, 14,
21 top, 30 bottom, 33 top; © Art Rickerby/Time Life Pictures/Getty Images: 27; © Herb Scharfman/Time Life
Pictures/Getty Images: 19; © Flip Schulke/CORBIS: 16; © George Walker/Getty Images: 36

Printed in the United States of America

1 2 3 4 5 6 7 8 9 08 07 06 05 04

TABLE of CONTENTS

Words that appear in the glossary are printed in **boldface** type the first time they occur in the text.

CHAPTER 1

THE GREATEST

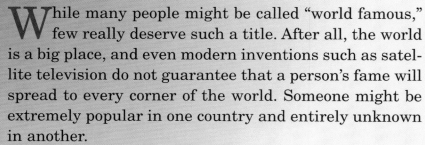

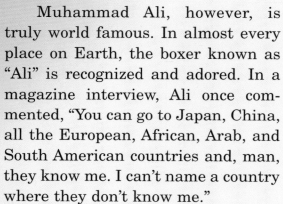

Muhammad Ali (right) defeats Ken Norton in a 1976 fight for the world heavyweight championship title.

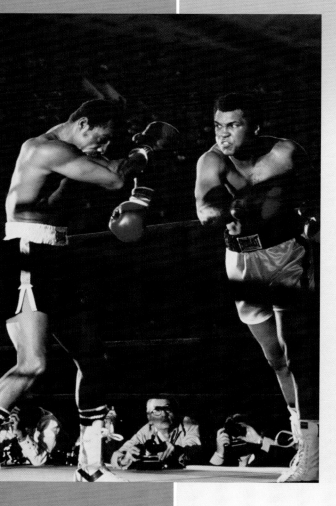

While many people might be called "world famous," few really deserve such a title. After all, the world is a big place, and even modern inventions such as satellite television do not guarantee that a person's fame will spread to every corner of the world. Someone might be extremely popular in one country and entirely unknown in another.

Muhammad Ali, however, is truly world famous. In almost every place on Earth, the boxer known as "Ali" is recognized and adored. In a magazine interview, Ali once commented, "You can go to Japan, China, all the European, African, Arab, and South American countries and, man, they know me. I can't name a country where they don't know me."

Ali first achieved acclaim for his boxing skill—he is one of the greatest boxers in the history of boxing. In the last century, however, there have been many gifted athletes, including boxers. What made Ali rise above them all, to become not just a successful boxer but one of the most popular figures of the twentieth century? The answer has to do with Ali's courage and conviction in the face of many obstacles, his deep spiritual beliefs, and his warm embrace of people of all stripes.

Ali first came to prominence in the 1960s, a turbulent period in the history of the United States. During this period, issues such as race and equality—as well as U.S. involvement in a civil war in South Vietnam—divided the nation's people, often pitting young against old and blacks against whites. Ali's boxing career was a wild roller-coaster ride that, in many ways, reflected the turmoil around him.

He began this career as Cassius Clay, a wise-cracking, poetry-spouting young black man from Louisville, Kentucky, who used his talent in the ring to leave behind **segregation** and poverty. Cassius Clay enjoyed great popularity. But when he adopted a new religion, joined an African American group known for its radical and often anti-white attitudes, and changed his name, he alienated much of white, mainstream society. Despite what some might have thought of him, however, he was still the heavyweight champion of the world, and he continued to hone his tremendous boxing skills. Then he refused the **draft** during the war in Vietnam, and he became an outcast. He was arrested for draft evasion and stripped of his title. Few people wanted to see him fight. It appeared that his once-promising career was finished.

But times changed, and so did people's attitudes toward Ali. His justification for refusing to serve in the war, on religious grounds, was ultimately upheld by the U.S. Supreme Court. Just as importantly, more and more people began to agree with his view that the United States should not be involved in the Vietnam War, and U.S. forces eventually withdrew from the conflict. As African Americans began to see some improvements in their lives, the struggle for **civil rights** became less intense, and racial tensions began to ease. The tough, determined Ali slowly worked his way back to the cham-

pionship title, earning the admiration and respect of all who watched him. He had never abandoned his beliefs, and in many places around the world, he had never lost his popularity.

By the time Ali retired from boxing, more than twenty years ago, he was a living legend. As always, however, he sought new challenges. Despite the effects of a debilitating disease, Ali became a goodwill ambassador to the world, using his fame and popularity to promote many important causes.

During his boxing career, Ali became famous for the boasts he made, before and after a fight. "I am the greatest!" he would often shout, to anyone who would listen. "I am the greatest of ALL time!" Today, many people around the world do consider Ali to be the greatest, and not just for his success in the ring. He has come to symbolize how important it is to fight for what you believe.

The Ancient Sport of Boxing

Boxing is one of the world's oldest sports. The ancient Greeks, for example, included a form of "bare-knuckles" (no gloves) boxing in their early Olympic games, which took place about 600 B.C. Modern boxing became more organized in the mid-1800s, when a British fan of boxing, or "fisticuffs," created a set of boxing rules, many of which are still used in boxing today. Called the "Marquess of Queensbury" rules, they prohibit kicking, biting, gouging, and other tactics. They also established the practice of dividing a match into a series of time periods, called rounds. The length and number of these rounds have varied over the years.

Boxing matches are held on a square, raised platform called the boxing ring. The sides of the square can be 18 to 24 feet (5.5 to 7.3 meters) long. Four padded ropes stretch along each side and attach to padded posts at each corner. The floor is usually covered by canvas that is stretched over several inches of padding. Boxers return to opposite corners of the ring between rounds. In boxing, the ring is sometimes called "the squared circle."

CHAPTER 2

BRINGING HOME THE GOLD

Cassius Clay was born on January 17, 1942, in Louisville, Kentucky. Clay's father, Cassius Marcellus Clay, Sr., was a sign painter, while his mother Odessa worked as a maid. The Clay family, which included Cassius's younger brother, Rudy, was not terribly poor. But the family was not well-off or even middle-class, and it had to contend with the racism and segregation that existed throughout the South at the time. Segregation in Louisville split the city into two worlds—one for white people and another for black people. In Louisville, blacks and whites used separate public facilities and institutions, such as swimming pools, parks, and schools. Blacks even used separate drinking fountains and restrooms. The neighborhood where Cassius lived was mostly black, and so was the school he and his brother attended. As an African-American boy growing up in Louisville in the 1940s and 1950s, Cassius could not swim in city pools or take a seat at the front of a city bus. In some white neighborhoods, he could not even look at a white person. At the time, it was not unusual for a black person to be chased out of a white neighborhood by hostile whites.

The two worlds created by segregation were by no means equal. In most cases, facilities and institutions in segregated black communities were inferior to those of white, mainstream society. Black communities often suffered from poor schools and housing and a lack of decent jobs. Like most blacks, young Cassius had little hope of escaping the despair of his segregated community. But

In the segregated South of the mid-twentieth century, African Americans were barred from using "white only" waiting rooms at bus and train stations. Most so-called "colored" waiting areas were uncomfortable and poorly maintained.

then he found a white man who was willing to cross the divide between the white and black worlds, and a life was opened up to him.

When Clay was twelve years old, his bicycle was stolen while he attended a fair at the Columbia Auditorium in Louisville. He reported the theft to police officer Joe Martin, who was working in the basement gym of the auditorium. Martin, who was white, supervised young boxers. He took the report, then offered Clay a chance to try boxing. According to Martin, Clay was "a little smart aleck," but the boy took immediately to the sport and showed great promise. Martin often had young boxers compete on a local television show called

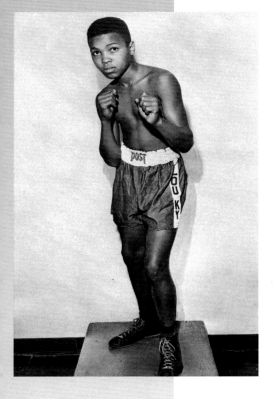

Twelve-year-old Cassius Clay strikes a boxer's stance.

"Tomorrow's Champions." Clay's appearances on this show were the first of thousands he would make on television.

In addition to Martin, Clay also trained with Fred Stoner, an African American boxing coach. Stoner helped Clay develop his unique boxing style, which emphasized speed and agility rather than punching power. He taught Clay that not getting hit was just as important as hitting. Clay learned to move his head, shoulders, and body to avoid as many punches as possible.

The young Clay's style proved to be a successful one. As a teenager, Clay won 100 of 108 fights and won six state Golden Gloves championships, which are amateur boxing tournaments for younger boxers held at the local, state, and national levels. Clay also won two Amateur Athletic Union national titles.

A NEW WAY OF TALKING

As Clay continued to hone his fighting skills, he also began shaping the outspoken, colorful personality that would set him apart from other athletes. At the time, most boxers were quiet men who rarely boasted and usually let their fists do their talking. Athletes in general rarely talked or acted in controversial ways, and black athletes were especially careful about their behavior. When Clay was a young man, black athletes were still relatively new in professional sports. The first black professional baseball player, Jackie Robinson, began playing for the Brooklyn Dodgers in 1947, and the first black players in professional basketball and football also didn't begin playing until the 1940s and 1950s. These black athletes could not risk antagonizing white sports fans, many of whom had not yet accepted the idea of black athletes in professional sports. Jackie Robinson, for example, set an example for all black professional athletes by never responding when taunted by racist white fans.

Jackie Robinson's behavior reflected the way many black people acted at the time. Particularly in the South, blacks often stayed silent about the injustices they faced, and whites counted on this silence. In many cases, black people did not protest against racism

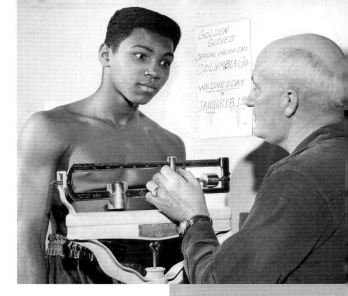

Joe Martin checks Cassius Clay's weight in this 1958 photo.

Golden Gloves

The Golden Gloves youth boxing tournaments began in Chicago in the 1920s and then spread to other major U.S. cities. Today, more than thirty cities hold annual Golden Gloves events for boys up to the age of eighteen. In addition to Muhammad Ali, many other top professional boxers got their start in the Golden Gloves, including Rocky Marciano, Sugar Ray Leonard, Evander Holyfield, Mike Tyson, and Oscar de la Hoya.

because they feared the reactions of whites. These reactions could be violent and even deadly.

Cassius Clay, however, was boastful, loud, and funny, both in and out of the ring. The young **phenom** made up rhymes about his fights and predicted in what round he would win. He loved to speak about himself, noting that he was "pretty" and his opponents were "ugly." A boxer named Allen Hudson, whom Clay defeated in 1959, partly inspired this "chatter," but Clay turned it into a new, original style of talking that was all his own. Soon, Clay's chatter would go international.

BRINGING HOME THE GOLD

In early 1960, Clay qualified as a light-heavyweight on the U.S. boxing team that would compete in the 1960 Summer Olympics in Rome, Italy. Although Clay was a talented, intelligent young man, his exposure to the wider world was limited. He was terrified of the long plane ride he would have to make to Italy, and Joe Martin spent several hours convincing him that he could not take the train to the Games. Clay even wore a parachute throughout the flight.

Once Clay landed safely in Rome, however, he quickly made himself at home. With his outgoing personality and wit, he became the unofficial leader in the athletes' Olympic Village. Once the competitions began, he made his name in the ring, too, defeating boxers from Belgium, the **Soviet Union**, and Australia. In a bloody and hard-fought final

Cassius Clay (right) defeats Gennady Schatkov during the 1960 Olympics in Rome, Italy.

match, Clay captured the Olympic gold medal by defeating veteran boxer Zbigniew Pietryskowsky from Poland.

Clay returned to the United States a hero. But he would soon learn that even Olympic gold did not buy racial equality.

Olympic Boxing

Boxing has been a part of the modern Olympic Games since 1904. Olympic boxing tournaments include competition in a wide range of weight classes. A tournament consists of a series of matches that each last three rounds of three minutes each. A single loss eliminates a boxer from the tournament. Olympic boxing is judged purely on the number of blows a boxer lands. Special boxing gloves with white panels over the knuckles are used, and points can only be scored by hitting the opponent on the head or torso with those white panels. Professional boxing matches, on the other hand, last anywhere from eight to fifteen rounds that each last three minutes. The winner of the match is decided by boxing experts who judge the match subjectively with a variety of criteria.

TARNISHED GOLD

Cassius Clay prized his gold medal. He later said that he "slept on my back all night while I wore it so I wouldn't have to lie on top of it." He never took it off, even when he walked through the streets of New York City on a trip there after returning from Rome.

His gold medal, however, did not bring him universal respect. Another color—that of his skin—still had the greatest impact on his life.

Back home in Louisville, Clay and some of his friends were refused service at a diner, one of many in the segregated city that would not serve African Americans. A scuffle broke out, and Clay fought off several attackers. The incident affected him deeply.

He had represented his country in the Olympics and won a gold medal, and yet he still had to contend with racial intolerance and hatred in his own hometown. He threw his medal into the Ohio River, which runs through the city.

In 1996 Ali received a gold medal to replace the one he threw into the Ohio River in 1960. He is pictured here kissing the replacement medal.

GOING PRO

Although Clay was bitter about the racism he had encountered when he returned from the Olympics, he knew that his future was in professional boxing. In late 1960, he turned pro, signing a contract with a group of white businessmen from Louisville who agreed to pay all of his training expenses in return for 50 percent of his winnings from boxing. They were certainly supportive of the young boxer, but their main goal was profiting from his skills by receiving part of his future prize money. With his first advance from the businessmen, Clay bought his parents a new Cadillac and renovated their home.

In Clay's first professional fight, which took place on October 29, 1960, he won a six-round decision against a boxer named Tommy Hunsacker. Clay's next step was to find a trainer, a man who could guide his career. Consulting with his father and his advisers, Clay eventually chose a small Italian man named Angelo

Dundee, who was based in Miami, Florida. When Clay arrived in Miami at the end of 1960, he and Dundee began one of the most successful partnerships in sports. Together, the young black man from the South and the grizzled old man from Italy would make boxing history.

Trainer Angelo Dundee (left) with Muhammad Ali in 1966

Professional Boxing

By the late 1800s, boxing had become enormously popular as a spectator sport, and the best fighters were well-known celebrities. In the 1920s, boxers such as Jack Dempsey, Gene Tunney, and Kid Gavilan were wealthy, famous figures. African American boxer Joe Louis was a popular champion before and after World War II.

By the start of World War II, boxing matches involved a lot of money and were becoming bigger and bigger spectacles. In some cases, organized crime influenced the outcomes of matches, with boxers being bribed (or threatened) to lose on purpose so that huge bets on the matches could be won. National and international boxing organizations helped make the sport of boxing more legitimate, and by the time Ali began fighting as a pro in the 1960s, boxing as a sport was regulated and mostly free of corruption. Greedy businessmen, however, did take advantage of some boxers.

Today, businessmen known as "promoters" put together most big fights. They arrange the matches between boxers, schedule the large arenas—such as Madison Square Garden—where the fights will take place, and negotiate the incredibly lucrative television contracts.

CHAPTER 3

CHAMPION!

Under Dundee's guidance, Clay's professional boxing career continued with one **knockout** after another. Dundee sought to arrange fights against a variety of opponents, from young boxers like Clay to older, more experienced fighters. He wanted to expose Clay to as many boxing styles as possible. Dundee knew that Clay would win these fights easily but would also learn from them.

Clay did win easily, and he gained press coverage as much for his bragging as for his boxing ability. He continued to make up rhyming poems that predicted when he would defeat his opponent. Before a 1963 fight against a boxer named Doug Jones, he told reporters:

Jones likes to mix,
So I'll let it go six.
If he talks jive,
I'll cut it to five.
And if he talks some more,
I'll cut it to four.

Although this particular prediction did not come true, most did. As Clay continued to win, his antics became more outrageous. He learned a few lessons from a professional wrestler named Gorgeous George, who had become famous for his wild hair, crazy costumes, and unending boasts. Clay realized that George's boasts and outlandish appearance, combined with his wrestling skill, drew crowds and made the wrestler a lot of money. So Clay began to boast even more, and he further

1963: "The Louisville Lip" accurately predicts that he will beat Henry Cooper in five rounds. Such boasting quickly became a big part of Clay's public image.

developed his light-footed, crowd-pleasing style in the ring. As Clay kept boasting and winning, he earned the nickname "The Louisville Lip."

Around this time, Clay used a phrase to describe his boxing style that would become his most famous. He promised that, in the ring, he would "float like a butterfly, sting like a bee."

TOUGHENING UP

As Clay was winning matches, he was also becoming tougher in the ring. He couldn't avoid every punch, and to become a champion, he would have to learn to take punishment as well as give it.

Dundee saw that his student was learning his lessons well during a fight with Sonny Banks in 1962. Banks, said Dundee, "hit him wit the finest left hook I'd ever seen. It would have floored King Kong. His [Clay's] eyes glazed over and like he was out of it and he hit the canvas [the floor of the boxing ring]. Then he sprang back up, bright-eyed and bushy-tailed, and he stopped the guy cold."

Another tough battle came against a British boxer named Henry Cooper.

Weighing in on Weight

Boxing is divided into different classes, which are based on a boxer's body weight. Boxers of similar weights are paired against each other to create fair and competitive matches. Cassius Clay fought as a light heavyweight in the Olympics and in the heavyweight class as a professional. Below is a list of weight classes (with the minimum weight, in pounds, for each class) used in boxing.

Class	Min. Wt. (Lbs.)	Class	Min. Wt. (Lbs.)
Strawweight	105	Junior welterweight	140
Junior flyweight	108	Welterweight	147
Flyweight	112	Junior middleweight	154
Junior bantamweight	115	Middleweight	160
Bantamweight	118	Super middleweight	168
Junior featherweight	122	Light heavyweight	175
Featherweight	126	Cruiserweight	190
Junior lightweight	130	Heavyweight	191 and above
Lightweight	135		

By the time of this 1971 fight against Joe Frazier (left), Ali had learned to take a punch.

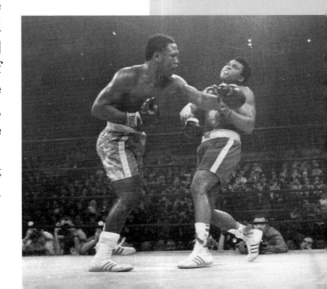

Clay's fame had spread to England, and the young boxer was invited to London to take on the British champ. Although Clay landed many punches against Cooper in the first four rounds, at the end of the fourth round Cooper stunned him with a sudden left. The time between boxing rounds is usually one minute, but because of a tear in his glove, Clay got a slightly longer rest. It was enough to let him recover to defeat Cooper— in the fifth round, just as he had predicted to an outraged British press before the fight.

Clay's combination of boxing skill and showmanship was bringing him more and more attention. He was getting close to realizing his goal: a chance to compete for the world boxing championship.

ANOTHER KIND OF FIGHT

Racial tensions in the South ran high in the mid-sixties, especially after the mysterious murders of three civil rights workers outside Philadelphia, Mississippi, in 1964. In this photo, police keep a close eye on civil rights supporters marching in Philadelphia.

While Clay fought in the ring, thousands of other African Americans began to mount a different struggle in the streets, protesting against racial inequality. By the early 1960s, the Civil Rights Movement, which had begun in the mid-1950s, was gaining strength. Led by black ministers such as Martin Luther King, Jr., African-Americans (as well as some sympathetic white supporters) were demonstrating in Southern cities against segregation laws. They staged sit-ins, marches, and boycotts, some of which were met with violence by police and white citizens. It was a tense and dangerous time in the United States. The country's centuries-old racial hostility was coming to a head, and the South was the focal point for much of the action.

In 1963, a protest march to Washington, D.C., ended with one of the most famous moments of the Civil

Rights Movement, when Dr. Martin Luther King, Jr., gave a televised speech to the thousands of protesters who had gathered in the nation's capital. King's speech inspired many American citizens, both black and white. But it also angered many other Americans, particularly in the South. Many of these Americans agreed with Alabama governor George Wallace, whose motto was "segregation then, segregation now, segregation forever."

LOOKING FOR LISTON

When King gave his famous speech in the capital, the heavyweight boxing champion was Sonny Liston. A tough, surly fighter, Liston

"I Have a Dream"

On August 28, 1963, with much of the nation watching on television, Dr. Martin Luther King, Jr., gave an impassioned speech about racial harmony, which he delivered on the steps of the Lincoln Memorial in Washington, D.C. Below is an excerpt of his speech:

"I have a dream that my four little children will one day live in a nation where they will not be judged by the color of their skin but by the content of their character.

I have a dream today.

I have a dream that one day, down in Alabama, with its vicious racists, with its governor having his lips dripping with the words of [segregation]; one day right there in Alabama, little black boys and black girls will be able to join hands with little white boys and white girls as sisters and brothers.

I have a dream today.

I have a dream that one day every valley shall be exalted, every hill and mountain shall be made low, the rough places will be made plain, and the crooked places will be made straight, and the glory of the Lord shall be revealed, and all flesh shall see it together.

This is our hope. This is the faith that I go back to the South with. With this faith we will be able to hew out of the mountain of despair a stone of hope. With this faith we will be able to transform the jangling discords of our nation into a beautiful symphony of brotherhood. With this faith we will be able to work together, to pray together, to struggle together, to go to jail together, to stand up for freedom together, knowing that we will be free one day."

had demolished the graceful Floyd Patterson in 1962 to claim the championship title. Liston could not have been more different than Clay. He had spent time in prison, he was not well-spoken, and his fighting style emphasized power, not grace.

At the time, Clay was not the official "number one contender," which is the fighter ranked just below the champion. But Clay didn't want to wait any longer, and he started a campaign to embarrass Liston into fighting him. He told reporters he would beat Liston. He even had his father paint a sign on a bus that read "The World's Most Colorful Fighter—Liston Will Go in Eight," and parked it in front of Liston's home. Reporters loved listening to the cocky young fighter, who called Liston a "big, ugly bear" and "a chump, not a champ."

Liston finally agreed to fight Clay. The champ lacked Clay's gift for language, and when asked how the fight would go, he simply said, "If he stands and fights, I'll kill him. If he runs, I'll catch him and kill him."

A NEW CHAMP!

The match was scheduled for February 25, 1964, in Miami. Most people believed Liston would easily defeat the young Clay, and the odds were 7 to 1 that Liston would win. Clay acted even crazier than usual at the prefight weigh-in, later saying that "Liston is a bully, and bullies are scared of crazy people."

It turned out that Liston should have been afraid. Clay's stunning speed in the ring made it impossible for Liston to land any good punches. For three rounds, Clay danced around the ring avoiding Liston, who became increasingly tired. Even in the fourth round, when something got in Clay's eyes and he had trouble seeing, Liston couldn't hurt the young boxer.

The fight went on, with Liston tiring and Clay dancing and talking and jabbing. At the start of the seventh round, the unthinkable happened. Liston refused to answer the bell, claiming a hurt shoulder. Clay won. He was the new heavyweight boxing champion of the world

Clay had defeated the mighty Liston. Once again, one of his rhyming predictions had come true. Before the fight, he proclaimed,

> *Yes, the crowd did not dream,*
> *When they laid down their money*
> *That they would see*
> *The total eclipse of the Sonny!*
> *I am the greatest!*

Cassius Clay shouted to the television cameras, "I shook the world! I shook the world! I'm king of the world! I'm pretty! I'm a bad man! I am the greatest!"

But then Clay did something even more astonishing than beating Liston in the ring. He announced that he had changed his religious faith and his name.

1964: An elated Cassius Clay (soon to be known as Muhammad Ali) shows his emotion after capturing the world heavyweight championship from Sonny Liston.

At a press conference the morning after the fight, Cassius Clay announced that he had abandoned Christianity and was now a follower of Islam. He had joined the Nation of Islam, an organization that was attracting many African Americans with its particular brand of Muslim beliefs.

Clay's announcement stunned both fans and the press. Although Islam was a major religion practiced in many parts of the world, the majority of U.S. citizens were Christians, and they knew little about this faith. For white, Christian fans in particular, Clay's announcement was a betrayal. They had once cheered for him, but many thought his rejection of Christianity was a rejection of them, too.

The young boxer's allegiance to the Nation of Islam was especially upsetting to white fans. The Nation of Islam, which was also known as the Black Muslims, had combined elements of Islam with its own particular ideas about race and the roles of blacks in the United States. Many of these ideas were controversial. The group sought to advance the cause

Ali (left) and his cornerman, Drew "Bundini" Brown

Ali's Crew

Although boxers are alone in the ring, they usually have a "crew" that provides support and guidance, both during a match and between fights. Like most boxers, Ali had a wide variety of people who helped him, in good times and bad. Along with head trainer Angelo Dundee, Ali's crew often included assistant and **cornerman** Drew "Bundini" Brown, photographer Howard Bingham, Dr. Ferdie Pacheco, cook Lana Shabazz, friend Herbert Muhammad, and others.

When Ali (third from right) visited Egypt in June 1964, he joined the local Muslims in prayer.

While attending a Muslim convention in 1966, Ali reads a newspaper featuring Elijah Muhammad's picture. Ali is surrounded by several Sisters of Islam dressed in the habit of their order.

of African Americans, but its message was openly hostile toward whites. According to the group's teachings, white people were "devils" who wanted to enslave all non-whites. The Nation of Islam argued that blacks needed to separate from white, mainstream society and develop their own society within the United States.

Cassius Clay had one more surprise for the world. He announced that he would no longer use his "slave name," Cassius Clay, but would instead be called Muhammad Ali. Clay was making the point that the last name he received at birth had originally come from a white, slave-owning family only a few generations before, and it was not the name used by earlier ancestors in Africa. His new name, Muhammad, was given to him by Elijah Muhammad, the Nation of Islam's leader. (Islam is based upon the teachings of the prophet Muhammad.)

The name Muhammad means "one worthy of praise" in Arabic, but praise was the last thing on most people's minds for the young man who now called him-

self Muhammad Ali. Newspapers refused to use the name, and television broadcasters likewise insisted on calling the boxer Cassius Clay. In fact, it would be years before the name Muhammad Ali would command the **adulation** and respect that it does today. During the next few years in Ali's life, he would face trials that would test his new faith.

The Nation of Islam

The Nation of Islam was founded in 1930 by a Detroit businessman named Wallace D. Fard. After Fard's mysterious disappearance in 1934, one of his followers, Elijah Muhammad, took over leadership of the organization. By the 1960s, the group had caught the attention of thousands of African Americans.

Many of the beliefs and practices of the group came from Islam, a major religion that was established in the seventh century A.D. Islam is based on the teachings of an Arabian named Muhammad. According to Islam, Muhammad is the prophet of Allah, the one true God, and he communicated Allah's will to the people. Muhammad's teachings are contained in the Islamic holy book, the Koran.

The Nation of Islam mixed some of Islam's basic beliefs with ideas about how African Americans should improve their lives. The group claimed, for example, that all blacks were really "Moors," or Muslims from Africa, and that years of Christian influence had caused black people to lose their Muslim identities. Blacks needed to create a new society, a homeland within the United States that would be separate from the white world. In this new society, blacks would achieve their true potential, returning to their Muslim roots.

In the 1970s, the Nation of Islam changed its name to the World Community of Al-Islam in the West. It downplayed the idea of blacks being separate from whites, admitting non-blacks and focusing more on traditional Muslim beliefs and practices. Some members of the organization, however, split off to form a new group. Led by Louis Farrakhan, this group took the original name Nation of Islam and supported the idea of blacks being separate.

TROUBLING TIMES

At the time of his press conference, Ali had been interested in the Nation of Islam for more than two years. He saw in the group a way for him to find his own path in the world. He understood that he had been recruited into the group for the status and attention he would give it. Ultimately, however, his choice to become a Muslim was a matter of personal faith, and it was not an effort to gain more celebrity.

ON TO AFRICA

One of the first trips Ali took as the new champion was a trip to Africa. In the African countries he visited, people greeted him like a conquering hero. For them, he was a black man who proudly proclaimed himself to be the king of the world, at least in boxing. Ali's boisterous, exuberant personality also helped fuel his popularity. After all, Sonny Liston was also African American, but his quiet, even sullen, personality was never one that many people could embrace.

Ali's name change and conversion to Islam also played a huge role in his tremendous popularity abroad. People in Islamic nations such as Egypt were particularly proud to see a boxing champion who was a follower of their faith—or at least a form of it.

The reaction of Muslims to Ali was noted by Malcolm X, a black activist who had inspired Ali to become a Muslim. Malcolm X had once been a Nation of Islam leader, but by 1964 he was the leader of a breakaway Black Muslim group. In his *Autobiography of*

Malcolm X, he wrote, "Apparently every man, woman, and child in the Muslim world had heard about how Sonny Liston...had been beaten in Goliath-David fashion by Cassius Clay, who then had told the world that his name was Muhammad Ali, and his religion was Islam and Allah had given him his victory."

Although Ali had the support of the growing American Muslim community, he was shunned by the white press. Almost overnight, his reputation went from that of a wise-cracking, poetry-spouting source of entertainment to that of an anti-American, anti-white outsider. He was also shunned by prominent black athletes, such as Floyd Patterson and Jackie Robinson, who did not want him to become such a divisive figure.

The Civil Rights Movement, meanwhile, continued to grow, and so did the divide between whites and blacks. For awhile, Ali had been one of the few figures who could cross that divide, appealing to blacks and whites alike. Whites enjoyed his great skills and his entertaining personality. Blacks loved his heroic success. But when Ali became a Black Muslim, many white fans believed he had turned against them.

Despite what many fans might have though about Ali, he did not entirely agree with the Nation of Islam. He believed in many of the group's teachings, but he was also uncomfortable with some of the more extreme statements of its leaders. As Ali would later say in a 1991 biography, "Color didn't make a man a devil. It's the heart, soul, and mind that counts."

Ali's attitude toward the Nation of Islam mirrored the tensions that were brewing within the

Some people in the United States felt threatened by Muhammad Ali (below) after he joined the Nation of Islam. They thought he had become anti-American and anti-white.

African Americans in Sports

In the first half of the twentieth century, African-Americans were rare on the national sports scene. African American boxers such as Jack Johnson and Joe Louis gained international acclaim, while baseball players in the Negro League enjoyed large, if mostly black, crowds. Before World War I, black jockeys won several important horse races. But there were no black athletes at all in sports such as baseball, football, and basketball.

After World War II, many people began to protest the lack of black athletes in U.S. sports. If African Americans had been allowed to fight for their country, why couldn't they also be given a chance to play sports? Slowly, black athletes began to emerge in professional sports. Black football players Woody Strode and Kenny Washington broke the "color line" in professional football in 1946, and Jackie Robinson joined Major League Baseball in 1947 as its first black player. In 1950, Chuck Cooper and other black basketball players brought integration to the National Basketball Association.

By the mid-1960s, black athletes were competing in many sporting events from which they had previously been excluded, but large pockets of racism remained. In some cases, for example, college teams in the South refused to play against other teams that had black players. The 1966 Texas Western University basketball team turned heads when it won the national title with an all-black team, defeating an all-white Kentucky team.

Muhammad Ali was not the only black athlete in the 1960s who was affected by the Civil Rights Movement and its struggle for African American equality. Like Ali, some of these black athletes—such as football superstar Jim Brown—spoke against racism in American society. But Ali's stand against racism was nonetheless considered bold and groundbreaking in a white-dominated society that was still getting used to seeing black athletes at the national level.

Today, African American athletes can now be seen competing—and winning—in just about every sport, with golf player Tiger Woods and tennis players Venus and Serena Williams excelling at sports traditionally dominated by white players. Athletic ability, not skin color, now determines how far a person can go.

organization. Some members argued that the group was becoming too radical and divisive, while others believed it should continue its blacks-only, anti-white message. As the most famous Black Muslim, Ali often found himself torn between these two sides.

A rematch between Ali and Liston should have been a major event. But Ali's new faith, new name, and new reputation had dramatically reduced his popularity. In addition, officials in many states feared a violent backlash against Ali and refused to host the fight. Finally, the small city of Lewiston, Maine, agreed to let the fighters meet. The first Ali-Liston fight had drawn national attention, with a huge crowd at the ring and a large television audience. But when the second Ali-Liston fight took place, in May of 1965, only a few thousand people attended.

Although few people showed up for the fight, its end was as stunning as the first Ali-Liston match. Halfway into the first round, Ali hit Liston with a hard right. Liston dropped to the canvas, and the referee counted him out. Ali had successfully defended his title, but his knockout of Liston generated a lot of controversy. Some people felt that Liston should have been able to get up before the referee counted to ten. Others argued that Liston "took a dive," falling to the canvas on purpose in order to lose. Ali's knockout blow became known as the

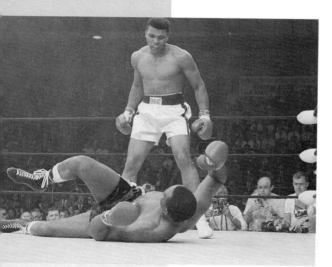

Title match of May 1965: Ali stands over Sonny Liston after throwing the "phantom punch"— the blow that gave Ali his stunning first-round victory.

"**phantom** punch," because many believed it had never landed. Despite the controversy, however, Ali had won the match. He was still the world champion.

In November 1965, Ali fought Floyd Patterson, the one-time champ who had been defeated by Sonny Liston. Patterson had come out strongly against Ali's new faith. In an interview for *Sports Illustrated*, he said, "I have nothing but contempt for the Black Muslims and that for which they stand." Ali took Patterson's comments very personally, and during the match he gave Patterson a terrible beating. Every time it seemed as if he could knock out Patterson, he stepped back and let the boxer recover. Then he hit him again. The fight, and Ali's fury, finally ended in the twelfth round. Many white boxing fans were sorry Patterson had not won and put the controversial champ in his place.

SUCCESS IN THE RING

Ali had one of his most successful years in the ring in 1966. Regardless of what the public thought of his religious faith and other aspects of his personal life, respect for his abilities as a fighter continued to grow.

Ali (right) savaged Floyd Patterson in November 1965.

That year, Ali defeated (in order) George Chavullo, Henry Cooper, Brian London, Karl Mildenberger, and Cleveland Williams. He fought some of these matches in Great Britain and Germany, and in these countries, he was a hero. For fans outside of the United States, Ali's new faith and new name did not have such a negative impact. In the United States, however, the country's racial turmoil did influence people's opinions of Ali, and white fans, as well as some black fans, continued to feel that he had turned away from the mainstream.

By 1966, civil rights was not the only controversial issue in the United States. In a small Asian country called South Vietnam, a civil war was raging between communist rebels, called the Vietcong, and the forces of the South Vietnamese government, which the United States supported. U.S. military involvement in South Vietnam had grown steadily since the civil war started,

Vietnam War

In the late 1950s, the United States became involved in a civil war in South Vietnam, a small country in Southeast Asia where communist rebels, known as the Vietcong, sought to overthrow the government of South Vietnam. The United States supported South Vietnam, while communist North Vietnam backed the Vietcong. At first, the United States only provided military advisors and equipment, but it eventually sent U.S. troops to South Vietnam to help South Vietnamese forces defeat the rebels. Several hundred thousand U.S. soldiers were ultimately involved in the conflict, which became known as the Vietnam War.

In the 1960s, as more and more people were drafted into military service and the number of U.S. soldiers killed or wounded in Vietnam kept rising, the conflict became a controversial, divisive issue in the United States. Many people began protesting U.S. involvement in the war, and this antiwar movement was greatly inspired by Muhammad Ali's refusal to fight. Ali became an important symbol of resistance. He appeared at numerous antiwar rallies, often on college campuses, and he also took part in antiwar demonstrations.

U.S. forces eventually withdrew from South Vietnam, with the last troops leaving in 1975. After the U.S. withdrawal, forces from North Vietnam defeated South Vietnamese troops. North and South Vietnam became one country, which is still ruled by a communist government today.

and by 1966 U.S. troops were being sent to the country. To provide the troops needed, the U.S. government relied on the draft. The number of U.S. soldiers killed in South Vietnam kept rising, and many people in the United States began to protest U.S. involvement in the war. A high percentage of the soldiers who were being sent to Vietnam were African American, a fact that further fuelled racial tensions. In the middle of this turmoil, Muhammad Ali received a letter that changed his life.

CALLED FOR THE DRAFT

As a young, healthy male, Ali was eligible for the draft. The boxer had tried, however, to have the U.S. government classify him as a conscientious objector (CO). A conscientious objector is someone who objects to serving in the military or fighting in a war for moral or religious reasons. Ali argued that his Islamic beliefs prevented him from fighting. But the U.S. government refused to classify him as a CO, and it sent him a letter telling him that he had been drafted.

On April 28, 1967, Ali reported to the enlistment center in Louisville to join the U.S. Army. A sergeant called out, "Cassius Marcellus Clay, step forward." But Ali refused.

By refusing, Ali was committing a federal crime: draft evasion. "I ain't got no quarrel with those Vietcong [communist rebels]," he said in a famous statement. "They never called me nigger." Ali opposed the war on religious grounds, but his decision was also a reaction to the ongoing racial struggle in the United States and to what he considered to be the racist policies of the U.S. government.

The reaction to Ali's decision was swift and harsh. Ali was tried for draft evasion, and in June of 1967 he was convicted. He was sentenced to five years in prison and was fined $10,000. Although he was allowed to remain free while he appealed his conviction to a higher court, his **passport** was taken away so he could not travel. In addition, the World Boxing Association (WBA) and the other boxing commissions stripped him of his heavyweight title.

Ali believed he was still the greatest boxer in the world, but now he could do nothing to prove it. He entered a troubled period in his career. In the United States, however, attitudes—about race, religion, the war in Vietnam, and Ali himself—kept changing. Eventually, Ali would rise to the top again.

His face set with determination, Ali is escorted from the induction center after refusing to be drafted into the U.S. Army in 1967.

Ali Speaks

In Thomas Hauser's 1991 book, *Muhammad Ali: His Life and Times*, Ali reflected on his refusal to be drafted and fight in the Vietnam War.

"Standing up for my religion made me happy. It wasn't a sacrifice. When people got drafted and sent to Vietnam and didn't understand what the killing was about and came home with one leg and couldn't get jobs, that was a sacrifice. But I believed in what I was doing, so no matter what the government did to me, it wasn't a loss."

CHAPTER 5

THE CHAMP RETURNS

Ali and Belinda Boyd after their wedding

Anti-war sentiment grew steadily in the late 1960s and early 1970s. At this rally in 1972, 30,000 anti-war demonstrators express their opinions in New York City.

In August of 1967, Ali married Belinda Boyd. She was Ali's second wife—he had been married briefly to Sonji Roi, from 1964 to 1966. Like Ali, Belinda was a devoted member of the Nation of Islam. But their first years together were a struggle, because Ali could not find a place that would let him fight. The boxing organizations had stripped Ali of his boxing licenses as well as his title. In theory, there were still plenty of venues where he could fight. But in practice, no one wanted to provide a place where a convicted "draft dodger" could earn money by boxing.

By the end of the 1960s, however, mainstream attitudes about the Vietnam War—and Muhammad Ali—were changing. As the war dragged on and there seemed no end in sight, more and more people began to question U.S. involvement in the conflict. For many, U.S. soldiers seemed to be dying for no good reason, in a distant and hopeless civil war that did not threaten the United States directly. Ali, who had stood firm on his beliefs about the war, eventually found that a growing number of American citizens shared his beliefs. In addition, many prominent African Americans who had not at first supported his conversion to Islam or his refusal to be drafted came around to his side again.

Elijah Muhammad was one African American who did not support Ali. The aging Nation of Islam leader had wanted Ali to stay out of the boxing ring for good, because he felt that Ali was glorifying himself and not the organization. Elijah was also not happy with Ali's rejection of some of the Nation's teachings about whites. He ultimately wrote that Ali was no longer part of the Nation of Islam, and he removed Nation of Islam guards from Ali's camp. Always his own person, Ali remained a devout Muslim, but he kept looking for a chance to box again.

RETURN TO THE RING

The city of Atlanta, which had a large African American population, finally allowed Ali a license to fight. On October 26, 1970, in Atlanta, Ali defeated Jerry Quarry. It was his first fight in three and a half years. During Ali's absence from boxing, a new champion had been crowned. Ali now set his sights on taking the championship belt back from "Smokin'" Joe Frazier.

Frazier, who had one of the fiercest punches in boxing history, was a tough, solid man who could take a punch better than most fighters and who seemed to enjoy dishing out punishment. Ali had lost some of his famous speed, and some wondered if he would have a chance against Frazier.

It was a chance he had to take. On March 8, 1971, "The Fight of the Century" was scheduled for Madison Square Garden, in New York City, between the returning hero and the reigning champ.

FIGHT OF THE CENTURY

Few sports events before or since have been as widely watched or anticipated as Ali-Frazier I, as the fight has become known. Madison Square Garden was packed with celebrities and boxing fans eager to see Ali fight for the title again, and a special television broadcast allowed more than three hundred million people in forty-six countries to watch the match.

Ali, feeling once again free to be himself, was back in action—with his mouth as well as his fists. He called Frazier ugly and stupid and claimed that he, Ali, was "the people's champ." Frazier, meanwhile, stewed quietly and channeled his anger into his boxing. Not long before the fight, he told *Sports Illustrated*, "I got a surprise for Clay. He loudmouthed so long and bigtalked so much that he got himself in a box. The man has to do or die. I think he's going to die."

Ali had his own prediction about the match, which he delivered in characteristic rhyme.

I'll be pickin' and pokin'
Pouring water on his smokin'
This might shock and amaze ya
But I'm gonna destroy Joe Frazier!

For the first nine rounds of the match, the two men circled each other. Ali danced away and jabbed, Frazier stalked and slugged. It was obvious that Ali had lost some of his speed, but would he still have enough to beat Smokin' Joe? During the 10th and 11th rounds, Ali slowed and Frazier began to land more punches. It was still a tight decision after the 14th round.

In the 15th round, however, Frazier's punching power finally caught up with Ali, when a left hook late in the round sent Ali down. Although Ali got back up, the blow had clinched the match for Frazier, and he won in a unanimous decision. For the first time as a professional boxer, Muhammad Ali had lost.

Ali might have lost to Frazier, but not long after the match in New York he won another fight. The U.S. Supreme Court struck down his conviction for draft evasion, accepting his Islamic beliefs as a legitimate reason for receiving conscientious objector status. Ali was now officially free of any legal problems. Just as importantly, the Court's decision had justified his decision to refuse to join the Army. Although some resentment might have still lingered in the general public, most fans seemed ready to embrace their hero again.

Eager cameramen practically scramble into the ring as Joe Frazier takes Ali down in their 1971 title bout.

BACK TO BOXING

In 1972 and 1973, Ali continued on his long comeback road. But he hit a major obstacle on that road when he fought big, strong Ken Norton. From the beginning of their match on March 31, 1973, Norton attacked Ali. Early in the fight, one of Norton's punches actually broke Ali's jaw. The former champ could have quit the fight, but he stayed in the ring, taking one hit after another. Norton won the 12-round fight easily, and after the match Ali underwent surgery to repair his jaw.

Poster advertising the Ali-Norton rematch of September 1973

Just as Ali's determination to stick to his religious principles eventually earned the world's respect, his performance against Norton earned him respect in the boxing community. "In losing to Norton, he actually won," wrote Dr. Ferdie Pacheco, Ali's physician. "He won the respect of his boxing peers. They knew from the Frazier fight that he was tough, from the Norton fight they learned how tough."

Ali returned in September to defeat Norton in a rematch. Up next was

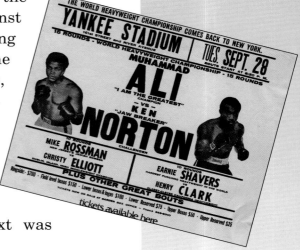

another fight with Frazier, but this time the match was not for the championship. Frazier had lost his title to young George Foreman in early 1973. Nevertheless, the Ali-Frazier rematch was a hugely anticipated fight.

The two men met in Madison Square Garden on January 28, 1974. This time, Ali was ready for the slugger. He controlled the fight from the beginning, jabbing Frazier repeatedly. Although both fighters were older and slower, it was an intense and thrilling fight, and it ended with a victory for Ali.

Once again, Ali's talent had put him in a position to become the champion. The next step in his journey back to the top was a fight with George Foreman. It would turn out to be one of the most remarkable matches of Ali's career.

Howard Cosell with Ali in 1974

Another Big Mouth

Throughout most of Ali's career, one sportscaster was closely linked to the champ: Howard Cosell. Working for ABC Sports, Cosell became almost as famous as Ali in the 1960s and 1970s. Cosell was a former lawyer who liked smoking huge cigars. He had a remarkable vocabulary, and unlike many announcers of the day, he "told it like it is." His honesty and his often-brutal opinions made him both loved and hated by many people.

Cosell interviewed Ali many times, and he was among the first journalists to use Ali's new name. Their loud and colorful interviews helped make both men stars. In one famous television interview, Ali mocked Cosell's hairpiece and pretended to swat at him, while Cosell sat back calmly and said "You wouldn't dare lay a hand on me." Cosell later went on to help make "Monday Night Football" a hugely popular sports broadcast. "If ever a broadcaster sought to bring sports out of the banal," he once said, "this, you see, is my mission."

VICTORY AND DEFEAT

With Joe Frazier defeated, Ali set his sights on regaining the heavyweight championship. The man standing in his way was big George Foreman, who had captured the title by defeating Frazier. The fight was to be held in Zaire (now called Congo). Mobutu Sese Seko, the president of Zaire, had promised to pay most of the $5 million that each boxer would receive for the fight. Called the "Rumble in the Jungle," the match became one of the most anticipated and talked-about fights in the history of boxing. It attracted celebrities from around the world to Zaire, a nation in the heart of Africa.

In Zaire, Ali proved his place on the world stage with his performance both in and out of the ring. Arriving in Zaire for the fight, Ali immediately became the local favorite. Everywhere he went, huge crowds greeted him with the cry, "Ali bumbaye! Ali bumbaye!" (Ali, kill him!). Ali's popularity in the United States might have suffered in the late 1960s, but in many other countries—especially countries in Africa and countries with predominantly Muslim populations—he had remained a hero. Now, in the 1970s, Ali had also become more popular in his own country. Racial tensions had lessened somewhat, and Ali's Muslim faith was no longer such a big issue for many fans. In Zaire, Ali was on the brink of worldwide acclaim.

Compared to Ali, Foreman came off as a sullen brute. While Ali went out to meet the people of Zaire, Foreman did not. Still, Foreman was bigger, faster, and seven years younger than Ali. Many in Ali's camp felt that Ali would suffer a disastrous loss.

Ali on Film

Filmmakers followed both Ali and Foreman throughout their stay in Zaire. The result was a documentary, *When We Were Kings*. Besides taking viewers on a behind-the-scenes tour of a big-time heavyweight fight, the film captures the intense adoration the people of Zaire felt for Ali. While the boxing action is exciting, even more compelling is Ali's interactions with the African people he meets. The movie shows how his qualities as a person, and not just his boxing ability, helped make him such a huge international hero.

In 2000, a full-length feature film about the fighter, *Ali*, was released. Starring the actor Will Smith as Ali, this dramatization of Ali's life has received great acclaim.

The fight was postponed for a month due to a cut Foreman received in training. Both fighters stayed in Zaire, and on October 30, 1974, the bell starting the first round finally rang. The fight began at four a.m. local time, so that fans in the United States, who were in a different time zone, could watch the fight in the evening. Ali immediately began using a controversial but successful new technique, huddling against the ropes with his forearms protecting his face and head. Foreman's mighty blows were not effective, and he soon tired. In addition to exhausting Foreman, this "rope-a-dope" technique allowed Ali to conserve his own energy. At the end of the eighth round, Ali threw one of the most powerful—and devastating—punches of his career. Foreman went down, and at the end of the count he did not get back up again.

According to most boxing experts, a heavyweight champion stood little or no chance of regaining his title once he had lost it. But Ali had proved the experts wrong. He was already a hero to millions of people around the world. Now, he was also the undisputed world champion.

Zaire, 1974: Huge crowds await the "Rumble in the Jungle." Here President Mobutu stands between Foreman (left) and Ali (right).

Though Ali was now firmly established as "the greatest," he still looked for new challenges. But while he took on, and defeated, some contenders in early 1975, his victories against these second-rate fighters left boxing fans—and the boxing business—wanting more. People began calling for a rematch with Joe Frazier, and Ali agreed to the fight. Both fighters were older now and past their prime boxing days. They still possessed powerful punches, however, and they would put on a show of strength that is still talked about today.

The fight was arranged for September 30, 1975, in Manila, the capital of the Philippines, a country in the South Pacific. Dubbed the "Thrilla in Manila," the match lived up to its name. Each man was determined to have this fight leave his final mark on the sport of boxing. Ali, with a win, could then retire from boxing having defeated all the other great fighters of his day. Frazier, for his part, needed a victory to salvage a career that had once been bright but had now faltered.

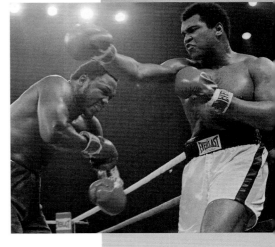

After beating Frazier in 1975, Ali (right) said their grueling match had been "the closest thing to dyin'."

On a brutally hot day—118° Fahrenheit (48° Centigrade)—the two fighters charged at each other from the start. There would be no "rope-a-dope" for Ali in this fight. The man known for his grace and speed stood toe-to-toe with one of boxing's strongest punchers. The two boxers traded terrible blows for round after round. For many fans, just watching the fight was a draining experience.

Finally, after the 13th round, with his mouth bleeding and his head ringing, Frazier refused to leave his stool. Ali had won by **technical knockout**. But although Ali had successfully defended his title, many people who saw the fight believed the pounding he took was a loss for him, too. Speaking about the match after it was over, Ali said, "It was the closest thing to dyin'."

THE END OF THE LINE

As his boxing career waned, Ali became a spokesperson for underprivileged children all over the world. Here he welcomes a young fan to his training camp in Deer Lake, Pennsylvania.

The fight with Frazier had taken its toll on Ali. He would not quit, however, though some thought he should. Whether Ali was fighting for money or for pride, or whether his handlers were sending him into the ring when he was reluctant to go, is not clear. What is clear is that after the third Frazier fight, Ali was not quite the same person.

From 1976 to 1978, Ali fought several long, hard fights. He won them all, including a 1976 decision over Ken Norton that many fans believed he did not deserve. These matches inflicted a lot of punishment on Ali's body, and Ali also injured his legs while battling a **Sumo** wrestler in an exhibition match. Sumo wrestlers are not boxers, and Ali was not a wrestler. The match was a show put on purely for profit. It was really not appropriate for an athlete as highly regarded as Ali.

Finally, in early 1978, a young fighter named Leon Spinks took advantage of the aging Ali, beating him in the ring to become the new heavyweight champion. But Ali showed his amazing resilience when he defeated Spinks in a rematch in September of 1978. In beating Spinks, Ali became the first man in boxing history to

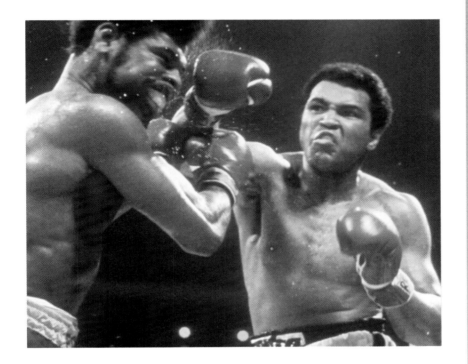

Ali (right) won the world heavyweight championship title for a record-setting third time when he beat Leon Spinks in September 1978.

win the heavyweight title three times. Ali officially retired in 1979, but he subsequently fought two more times, which were both embarrassing losses. His last fight in the ring came in 1981.

Although Ali's days as a boxer were over, he now had another battle to face. As he had done throughout his life, he took on this struggle with grace and courage.

Bouncing Back

Ali was the first fighter in boxing history to claim the heavyweight title three times. He won his first title in 1964, with his defeat of Liston; his second in 1974, when he beat George Foreman; and his third in 1978, when he won against Leon Spinks in a fifteen-round decision.

In 1996, Evander Holyfield became the first boxer to match Ali's record. Holyfield defeated Mike Tyson to earn the heavyweight title for the third time.

Joe Louis, the "Brown Bomber," holds the record for defending a heavyweight title the most times. From 1937 to 1949, Louis defeated twenty-five challengers.

CHAPTER 7

THE FIRE STILL BURNS

Three years after his last fight in 1981, Muhammad Ali was diagnosed with Parkinson's syndrome. Similar to Parkinson's disease, the condition is caused by the brain's inability to process a chemical called dopamine. This chemical helps control muscle function, and a person with Parkinson's syndrome often trembles, shakes, and has trouble walking and talking. Many medical experts believed that Ali's boxing career—especially the harsh punishment he endured in his last handful of fights—was the cause of his condition.

Despite his condition, Ali was eager to take on new challenges. Following his 1979 retirement announcement, Ali told the *Washington Post*, "Boxing was the dressing room—a preliminary to the big fight—for humanity, racial justice, freedom and human rights." Guided by his Muslim beliefs, Ali began using his celebrity and his influence to help bring about change all over the world. Ali commanded great respect among a large number of people—black and white, Muslim and non-Muslim—for staying true to his convictions. He became more than just a boxer.

Ali has nine children, some of whom are athletes. His daughter May May (above) is a cyclist. After divorcing Belinda Boyd in 1977, Ali married Veronica Porche. The marriage ended in 1986, and that year Ali married his current wife, Lonnie Williams.

A NEW ROLE FOR THE CHAMP

In 1980, U.S. president Jimmy Carter, recognizing Ali's positive reputation around the world, had sent Ali on a

goodwill mission to Africa. The United States planned to **boycott** the 1980 Summer Olympics to protest the invasion of Afghanistan by the Soviet Union, and Carter wanted Ali to rally support for the boycott. The trip did not bring the support Carter had wanted, but Ali was able to see that his popularity allowed him to speak out on issues he believed were important. In spite of the effects of Parkinson's syndrome, Ali began touring the world promoting peace and harmony.

In the wake of the terrorist attacks on September 11, 2001, Ali was one of the first people to be heard on the subject of Islam. Although some of his statements to the press have been disputed, he clearly spoke out for peace and understanding. Ali defended his Muslim faith as one of peace and proudly called himself "an American and Muslim."

Ali continues to travel the world, sometimes for as much as two hundred days a year. He lends his famous name to causes he supports, from food relief to adoption. Although Parkinson's syndrome has slowed Ali's speech, robbed his face of expression, and made most movements difficult, he carries on.

1998: The former boxer announces the formation of the Muhammad Ali Center in Louisville, Kentucky. The Center's mission is to "preserve and share the legacy and ideals of Muhammad Ali, to promote respect, hope, and understanding, and to inspire adults and children everywhere to be as great as they can be."

Ali with his daughter Laila, who is a professional boxer. Laila's career is young, but she has been undefeated in her first sixteen matches.

THE WORLD WATCHES ONE MORE TIME

In 1996, Muhammad Ali made a memorable appearance at the Summer Olympics in Atlanta, Georgia. During the opening ceremonies, the Olympic flame is lit, and it burns throughout the

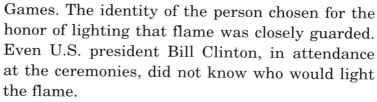

Athlete of the Century

In 2000, to celebrate the first year of a new millennium, ESPN, the national cable TV network, gathered hundreds of sports experts to help decide who were the greatest athletes of the twentieth century. The debate raged for months, and slowly the top fifty were revealed on television, in magazines and newspapers, and on the Internet. As the countdown neared the final few, many wondered who would be number one. Would it be Michael Jordan? Babe Ruth? Jim Thorpe?

In the end, the choice was obvious. The network selected Muhammad Ali as the Athlete of the Century. *Sports Illustrated* and *USA Today* also gave Ali this honor.

While thousands cheer, Muhammad Ali lights the Olympic flame at the 1996 Summer Games.

Games. The identity of the person chosen for the honor of lighting that flame was closely guarded. Even U.S. president Bill Clinton, in attendance at the ceremonies, did not know who would light the flame.

At the stadium where the opening ceremonies were held, former Olympic gold medalist Janet Evans carried the official torch on the last leg of its journey. It was now ready to be handed to the person who would light the Olympic flame.

When Ali emerged as that person, the audience in the stadium erupted in a long, sustained ovation. Millions of people around the world watched as Ali held out the torch with a shaky, unsteady arm. His face, once so expressive, was an emotionless mask. Yet he proudly held the torch aloft before slowly lowering it to light the flame.

Ali's lighting of the Olympic flame at the 1996 Summer Olympics is widely regarded as one of the most touching moments in the history of sports. During his long career, Ali had lit a flame in many

Muhammad Ali was designated a United Nations Messenger of Peace in 1998. Acting in that role, he visited Afghanistan in late 2002. He is shown here visiting an Afghan girls' school to show support for education for girls and women.

people's hearts. For some people it was a flame of adoration, while for others it was a flame of contempt. On that day in 1996, however, Ali lit a different kind of flame, one that most of the world will remember him by—a flame of peace and togetherness for all.

He was, he is, he always will be, "The Greatest."

Ali Speaks

Not long after the terrorist attacks on the World Trade Center and the Pentagon on September 11, 2001, Muhammad Ali was once again looked to as a spokesman for his beliefs. As it became clear that Muslim extremists were responsible for the tragedy, Ali, though his speech was slurred by Parkinson's, felt compelled to speak. After visiting the World Trade Center site, he said, "What's really hurting me [is that] the name Islam is involved, and Muslim is involved, and causing trouble and starting hate and violence. Islam is not a killer religion. Islam means peace. I couldn't just sit home and watch people label Muslims as the reason for this problem."

Ali's words helped some people focus on the fact that the enormous majority of Muslims in the world believe, as he does, in peace, and that the actions of a few should not be used to judge an entire religion.

TIMELINE

1942	Cassius Clay is born on January 17 in Louisville, Kentucky
1954	Begins boxing at local gym
1960	Wins Olympic gold medal in light heavyweight category
1963	Dr. Martin Luther King, Jr., delivers his "I Have a Dream" speech on August 28
1964	Defeats Sonny Liston to become heavyweight champion of the world. Joins Nation of Islam and takes new name, Muhammad Ali
1967	Refuses to join U.S. Army and is prosecuted for draft evasion. He is also stripped of his heavyweight title and licenses to box
1971	Loses to Joe Frazier in New York City; U.S. Supreme Court overturns his conviction for draft evasion
1974	Defeats Frazier in rematch; defeats George Foreman in Zaire, once again capturing heavyweight title
1975	Vietnam War ends; Ali wins another match with Frazier, the famous "Thrilla in Manila" fight
1978	Loses fight and title to Leon Spinks in February, then recaptures heavyweight title by defeating Spinks in September
1979	Announces his retirement from boxing
1980	Sent to Africa as a goodwill ambassador by U.S. president Jimmy Carter
1981	Fights his last match, against Trevor Berbick
1984	Diagnosed with Parkinson's syndrome
1996	Lights torch to begin Summer Olympics in Atlanta, Georgia

adulation: extreme admiration.

boycott: protesting against an organization or government by refusing to buy certain products, use certain services, or be involved in certain activities, in order to promote change.

civil rights: the basic rights belonging to every citizen in a country.

cornerman: in boxing, an assistant who works with the boxer between rounds when the boxer returns to his stool in the corner. A cornerman provides the boxer with water, medical aid, advice, and encouragement.

draft: another name for selective service, which is the U.S. government's selection of young people to serve in the armed forces. The draft was in effect throughout the 1960s and ended in 1973.

knockout: a boxing victory that results when an opponent is knocked down by a punch and is still unable to get up after the referee counts to ten.

passport: a document issued by a country's government to its citizens, which allows them to travel through foreign countries and return to their home country.

phantom: something that can be seen but does not have a physical presence, such as a ghost.

phenom: a person who shows exceptional ability at something and achieves a high level of success very quickly.

segregation: a system in which people of different races or backgrounds must use separate facilities and institutions, such as schools, restaurants, hotels, water fountains, and swimming pools.

Soviet Union: a former communist nation that consisted of Russia and neighboring republics in northwest Asia and Eastern Europe. The Soviet Union was established in 1922, after World War I. It broke apart in 1991.

Sumo: a form of wrestling that originated in Japan and involves giant wrestlers. The two opponents grapple in a small ring of stones, and a match ends when one wrestler succeeds in pushing the other wrestler out of the ring.

technical knockout: a boxing victory that results when a referee or other boxing official stops a fight because an opponent is still standing but is not physically able to continue.

TO FIND OUT MORE

BOOKS

Gordon, Randy. *Muhammad Ali*. New York: Grosset & Dunlap, 2001.

Jordan, Denise M. *Muhammad Ali: Meeting the Champion (Meeting Famous People)*. Berkeley Heights, N.J.: Enslow Publishers, 2003.

Latimer, Clay. *Muhammad Ali. (Journey to Freedom)*. Chanhassen, Minn.: The Child's World, Inc., 2000.

Myers, Walter Dean. *The Greatest: Muhammad Ali*. New York: Scholastic, 2001.

Penney, Sue. *Islam (World Beliefs and Cultures)*. Portsmouth, N.H.: Heinemann Library, 2001

Rummel, Jack. *Muhammad Ali (Black Americans of Achievement)*. Broomall, Pa: Chelsea House, 1989.

Tessitore, John. *Muhammad Ali: The World's Champion (Impact Biography)*. Danbury, Conn.: Franklin Watts, 1998.

INTERNET SITES

International Boxing Hall of Fame
www.ibhof.com
Visit this site to learn about Muhammad Ali and many other important boxers.

Muhammad Ali Center Site
www.alicenter.org
The Muhammad Ali Center is scheduled to open in Louisville, Kentucky, in 2004. It will be an international cultural and educational institution that preserves and shares the legacy of Muhammad Ali. This web site has information about both the center and Ali.

Muhammad Ali Official Site
http://www.ali.com/
This site has a wealth of material about the fighter, including a biography, frequently asked questions, and letters from fans.

Muhammad Ali: The Making of a Champion
www.courier-journal.com/ali/index.html
This site follows Ali's career with stories and photographs.

INDEX

INDEX *(continued)*

About the Author

James Buckley, Jr., has written more than thirty-five books for young readers on a wide variety of sports, including baseball, football, hockey, the Olympics, and soccer. A former editor at *Sports Illustrated* and NFL Publishing, he has written biographies of Troy Aikman, Peyton Manning, Bill Bradley, and Roberto Clemente, as well as the *Trailblazers* book on tennis stars Venus and Serena Williams.